# Thank You
# for Your Patience
# & other ways to say
# exactly what you mean

# Thank You
# for Your Patience
# & other ways to say
# exactly what you mean

Kelly M. McMinn

gatekeeper press
Columbus, Ohio

Title: Thank You for Your Patience
& other ways to say exactly what you mean

Published by Gatekeeper Press
2167 Stringtown Rd, Suite 109
Columbus, OH 43123-2989
www.GatekeeperPress.com

ISBN (paperback): 9781662912283

# CONTENTS

## III. A word about what love might be like

For my Mother, my biggest fan

*Wait; wasn't ready...*

*k, now I'm ready*

# I.
# Appetizers

## Curriculum Vitae

Human, I suppose.
Part wolf. Probably.
Part something else. Maybe.
From some place where the sun is content
behind a layer of frosty stratus,
and the temperature that is scientifically
concluded as cold.
is traditionally, culturally, and virtually
accepted as warm.
Part Jazz,
something slow and groovy,
something that Jessica Rabbit might sing to,
at least, I might like to think so.
Part Rock, but the part just before hair got too big
and music got too computery.
Part Fantasy. Part Science Fiction. With dashes of Dystopia.
Part whiskey. Smooth,
Rough edges to finish.
Part Rum.
Deep, dark amber, uncorked, then poured over a giant amethyst
ice cube.
Sipped, until ultramarine coats the inside of your mouth,
and threatens to push through your eyes,
daring you to wax entirely too poetic.
Giving voice to entirely too many adverbs.
There is a fault in my code.
A glitch in my computery system.
For I have become systematically aware of things
that I should have known all along.
Things that require an upgraded bandwidth.

The darkness in me recognizes the darkness in you.
It knows the love you need just to stay afloat.
It's the darkest of us that love the deepest.
We know the cost to accept the burden.
Thank you for listening, if you felt yourself theoretically moved,
donations will be accepted at the door on your way out.
Like, Comment, Subscribe, Shit on the Floor, Buckle up, Get
Schwifty.

## C.V. II

Male. 30. White.
Non-hispanic. A statistic. Still not voting. Get mad. Sue me. I don't
care who wins.
"yOu sHoUlD-"
I don't.
Male. 30. White.
Likes cats. candles. cookies, and a hot shower
amongst a lotta other things that he probably wouldn't tell you
about,
and some would call that toxic. He would call it preserving the
mystery.
Male. 30. White.
Has a gym membership. Hates the gym. Goes anyway.
Because when you're growing up and "fat" equals "disgusting"
You don't want to be disgusting. Thus preserving the vanity.
Male. 30. White.
Probably Scottish -ish.
Would currently rather be Scottish than American.
Fuck a fuckin' pair of pants.
Would rather be a kilt-wearing, wild-haired Eccentric.
Male. 30. White.
Is kind of already a kilt-wearing, wild-haired Eccentric.
Eccentric, in this case, a word meaning a crazy person that makes
things.
A creative.
Also, fuck pants.
Male. 30. White.
Paints. Makes music. Does all the, y'know, the sensitive art shit.
Writes poetry.
Will cry if he feels like the colors, words, notes,

hit his little slice of atmosphere just right.
Male. 30. White.
Insensitive. Not Inconsiderate. Been accused of racism.
sexism.
And being a mutha fucken creep.
Each, thankfully, only once, to his knowledge
but after each accusation, vehemently, self-consciously,
and not without a bit of haste,
has taken infallible mental, and external inventory to the contrary.
Male. 30. White.
Is not known to initiate a conversation due to these allegations.
Nothing past "Hey," anyway.
And never at a place where alcohol is distributed, and consumed.
That's just creepy.
Male. 30. White.
Smokes
cigars, and pairs them with whiskey, rum, or tequila with lime
because some flavors are meant to be savored together.
Eats
pussy for the same reasons, mostly.
Male. 30. White.
His first instinctual reaction to "I'll miss you." is
"No, the fuck you won't"
because he is not convinced.
Male. 30. White.
Coated in a shell of brutal honesty, is still just a fucken statistic. And
that's ok.

## Somewhere that feels like home

I hear it. It lives in my mind. Rent free. But it takes me to somewhere
In the distance. Over the cliffs. The arctic breeze carries the tune.
It flies over waves that crash against ancient granite.
A stirring. In my blood. Something ancient like the sea against the stones.
The tune rolls on sea air, and plays with the fingertips
of grass fields where wolves hunt.
It echoes still through the waves providing its chorus.
Gliding over villages singing about Molly Malone
And through a wooden door held on cast iron hinges forged by the blacksmith.
Who is still the blacksmith after generations.
"I'll have a pint of the black stuff," and my bartender smiles. My accent is wrong.
But my face says that somewhere down the line, the drunk English girl who kept yelling 'Tipperary' at me from behind my bar back home might've been on to something.
For posterities sake, he asks where I'm from. I sigh, and that's all the answer he needs. He laughs. A massive laugh. Then he asks my name. I tell him and he says
"Boyo, coulda fooled meh oot the gaet"
The strings fade in. This time, something new from the corner of the pub.
Something that reminds me of voluptuous, wild, red curls, on an even wilder girl.
The highland air whips clouds of mist from her icy blue eyes.
She's the one who tells me to stay. And to experience the end of life as I know it.
I say I might, though I know I shouldn't be so goddamn indecisive.
It's the air, you see, the air just as fresh as her giggle,

that tugs at the hem of my black t-shirt
The air here, not filled with the smog, and shards of fragile promises
or the glittering of shattered dreams.
No 'know-a-guy-who-knows-a-guy' or 'pay-to-play.'
Only life, fresh greens, and bright blues.
Ferries to the market and pints when the day is out.
Brought together by four strings.
No one would miss me for the right reasons if I left.
Watching the sunset burn from a different layer of the horizon
Singeing pages of a journal filled with words of lost love
Too early mornings, and stolen baggage. The city wouldn't long
for me.
And I quite prefer that.

## When you're young

There should be a place you could walk to
When you're young
A place with hills, gauntlets for the bike with one speed to run
(as fast as your legs can move it)
and one brake
(better hope the wires don't snap)
Hills that are narrow, and paved from a time when gas was cheaper,
that are cracked, and split by roots older than the lake on the next
block
that was filled by some local government
(can you swim to the dock?)
I learned to sail on that lake.
I learned confidence on that lake.
But on those hills,
Easing off the brake,
On those hills, I was Achilles.

**Level Up**

In an effort to rebel against everything I had learned to be
I became unapologetically myself.
Where everything is smooth, and silky
except the edges.
Little rough. Little frayed.
but that shit adds character.
You see, the thing about knowing exactly what you are
is that there is still a different version of you in everyone's mind.
Which can only mean one thing.
You. Are. Infinite.

*Is he monologuing?*

## Colors I.

Everyone has a color.
I don't know what you would be if you didn't, but you should
pick one. Mine? Blue. My color is blue. Ultramarine to be exact.
A glowing blue. A blue that makes the eyes feel fuzzy and warm.
The type of warmth you get when your body has acclimated to
surrounding
water, and you don't want to get out. A blue that cradles and
protects.
The blue that's dark enough to hide secrets. Where mystery can float
in black wisps
like tentacles of an octopus on the ocean floor. Or like wings on a
manta ray
in the open water where the bluest of whales sing to each other.

Everyone has a color. I've met red. Red and I have our
disagreements,
but the shades of violet we make when we blend (between sheets)
and in
our minds are vast. We discover things about each other, Red and I.
I've had Purple, not grape (even the word seems as artificial as the
flavor)
But lavender, blended with merlot, was this purple. She was one of
my very favorites.
The coolness of our colors mixed like the last
vibrato of an evening sunset, or the first chord of a sunrise
symphony.
At least, they used to.

I've met most of the colors attached to the humans. Too many to list.
Each blends in one way, or another,
and I've found my people are the coolest of colors

(my fur does not do well with the heat)
Emerald. Aqua. Turquoise. Viridian. Cerulean. Lapis, Violet. Cobalt.
Colors of waves in a waning sunlight.
Revealing the Darkness. These are mine. They stay with me.
Those and any on the spectrum.
Everyone has a color. I want you to be mine.
Let yourself get tossed in my waves.

## Zoned

Sometimes, it's staring out a window into the void
that levels me.
I sit. I stare.
I shuffle those insatiable scrolls of parchment held in ancient
bookshelves
stacked with dust, lit by candles, and a glowing fireplace.
Flanked by more shelves volumed with books,
and tables stacked with horns of ale, and tea, and coffee.
The morning's breakfast spread.
Chaperoned by one raven, and one black cat,
curled on a plush rug, in front of the fireplace.
I stay in that place. In my mind.
And all you see is the glazing of my stormy eyes
as grey thunderclouds form.

## Lo-Fi

I really love how some music.
makes me feel like I want to close the blinds,
and pretend that the grey
sifting through the cracks is just rain clouds.
Makes me feel like I want it to pour. Always.
Darkened skies, and clouds that invite you to shiver.
As if that were a bad thing.

## Y' know?

It's just nice to know
that there are people
who laugh
with me
at things
that others fight about.

**Discount Hemingway**

You asked, so let me tell you the whole sad story.
At one point, Hollywood was my dirty, sweltering Paris.
The movable feast was a traffic jam on the 101
on a Tuesday in mid-July.

## West Coast Sentiment

Today I surfed to work
on waves of concrete
in a city that nobody wants to admit
scares them like the ocean.

**write me a song about being**

Over-caffeinated.
Under-stimulated.
and still doin' alright.

## I'm trying not to stare but

Would you think it crazy if I said
that I had a dream about you?
It's just that I can't remember your name.
Maybe it's all in my head or
your eyes are looking my way.
I know I may not know you
but a part of me
Is wondering if you'd
let me fit your hair in the
spaces between my fingers.
Don't worry.
I wouldn't think
to say that out loud.

**Not alone**

Everyone feels. Terrified. Hopeless. Clueless.
Everyone. At least once. If they tell you they haven't
they're lying.
And
well,
Maybe we're all just meant to be here
for everyone else
In those moments
when we don't
feel clueless, hopeless, terrified.
Maybe it's in those moments
when we are emboldened by the fact that,
at one point or another,
in our early adolescence we chose
to Rage
Against the dying of the light,
instead of fold inward like an anemone.
That we are called to
obligated to
destined to
Show the human across from us, at the table, sipping their tea
and
shifting their eyes
that you're allowed to think life is terrifying.

**Colors II.**

Life happens to us in shades of colors
along a spectrum we are not entirely aware of.
The cool colors.
The colors that speak of rain.
Nights. So close to black.
But maybe not cool enough.
To be so mysterious.
Black.
is the coolest color, of course.
Or is it the warmest? Only obsidian.
the blackest black.
Is formed from the hottest hot. Is it not?
The warm colors.
The colors that tell you to remember
your passion, your lust, your fire
Colors.
The right shade can be just enough to catch my breath.
The right shade can be just enough to give me hope.

## The philosopher's laugh

I want to laugh
like philosophers laugh
at themselves
when they explain
how we are everything
and nothing
at the same time.

## Chaos

If everything was good,
and peaceful,
and harmonious
would we long for chaos?
Are the edges of humanity so important?
the walled off little slice
of suburban delusion?
If you strain your ears
you can hear the screaming.

**In the hours before a shift**

You walk around with a book in your hand
just to make the first sip of coffee seem less menial.
Then It's reading Bukowski,
listening to Bossa Nova
and staring at a blank canvas
when you realize you may have too much.
You're drinking coffee from yesterday.
Staring at a half-finished painting
of a girl that does her no justice.
You'll make a hundred bucks at a bar shift tonight
and you'll call yourself an artist.
then most other times
You'll wish you were in an airport.
Reading. Waiting.
To go.
To be.
Somewhere else.

## Time well filled

Is time ever wasted sitting in a parked car finishing a song?
No, and anyone who tells you otherwise
Isn't worth the breath it would take
to prove them they're wrong.
So, here's to
singing alone in the car
when the guy who cut you off
pulls up next to you.
and here's to
good ramen before your next paycheck.
and here's to
the first sip of the first pour
from a new bottle of whiskey that
you didn't realize
was going to turn into your new favorite.

## finally

I like to think living to the fullest means
playing a song a million times
then after a while
finally hearing it for the first time.

## What if

our words are only
Images
&
Emotions
Melting the insides of our hearts,
until we're empty
like the inside of a guitar that only
Sings. Shouts. Shreds. Slides. Speaks.
when touched.

## beats the alternative

I see the world in brush strokes and blends,
I don't think I'll go back to whatever I saw before
but
I think. I think.
Painting until I can't see straight
is a welcome result to the alternative.

# II. Advice, maybe:

*as far as this section is concerned*
*it would be safe to assume*
*I'm not the one to come to*
*for advice.*

## Original Copy

Who's to say you're not admired from afar
for the quirks, the flaws, the scars, the blemishes,
that make you irrevocably, and originally human.
Who's to say that you're not everything
someone else wants
to have. to be.
to take a bite out of.
Who's to say your primordial calligraphy
isn't worth keeping a record of.
Well,
not you, for starters.

**Reclusiveness is part of the creative process, now fuck off**

Do not keep company with many people,
there is less chance for things to go wrong this way.
But if you must,
at least keep company with those who have the same taste in art.

## Mostly Jim Carrey

"You have to do what you don't like;
You have to be uncomfortable because
a predictable future is already the past.
What do they need that your talent can provide?
Find peace.
Unstrap the armour.
Decide, not out of fear, but out of love.
To become what the world didn't know it needed.
You can fail at what you don't want,
so you might as well take a chance at what you love."

**Thank You For Your Patience**

replaces "I'm sorry I'm late but…"
but what if you're not sorry?
What if your tardiness does not warrant an apology?
what if you were, in fact, compelled
To arrive at whenever you saw fit?
"I'm sorry. I'm sorry. I'm so sorry."
even when you're not.
Why is it not;
"I'm sorry, I know I'm late, I didn't want to come."
The thing is, you're not. You're not sorry.
"I'm sorry I'm late, I can't seem to manage my time very well"
Acceptable.
But you should already know that you're going to have to shower
after jacking off for the third time that day,
and you should be able to adjust accordingly.
You're sorry?
I'm not convinced.
"I'm sorry I'm late, traffic was so bad!"
r e a l l y?...
Instead, maybe try
"Thank you for your patience…"
Try.
(It's neither discriminatory to discuss reality, nor is it cruel to be
honest.)
Try.
"Thank you for your patience, I've been working on my time
management habits, I've failed this time,"
"Thank you for your patience, I, uh, well, my shower time needs to
truncate in one way or another."

"Thank you for your patience, I would've been here earlier, but I found myself emotionally compromised at 2:17 in the morning, got lost somewhere between self-deprecation, and a jug of accelerant that I almost used to ignite every bridge between me, and actual human connection.

Instead, I set my GPS to take the scenic route. Had to put 'er in low gear over a couple whiskey-soaked journal pages, but, you know, I guess, well, here I am."

"Thank you for reading, I would like to know why you disagree"

"Thank you for laughing, I've really been working on my delivery."

"Thank you for listening." Thank you for listening.

"Thank you for enduring my mildly evocative cruelty, I appreciate your patience."

## An Ode to the Poets of My Generation

Why, Poet?
Do you scream into the microphone? Are you convinced your
amplified voice will carry far enough to change the minds of those
who choose to hear nothing but the shuffle of cash inside bonded
leather wallets?
Bonded leather. A lie. Do you know what "bonded leather" is? The
leftovers, the leather pellets. The strips and cuts that didn't make it
into the project. Snipped off. Discarded. Fodder. Then melted and,
well…
We're getting off topic.
Why, Poet?
Do you take the *deep, *dramatic, *Breath, *Between, *Lines,
*Stanzas, *phrasings
to increase your *oh *so *turmoiled *delivery *from the *depths *of
your *tortured
*artistic *Soul
Breathe, Poet.
Then whisper what you really want.
(You wish it would all. just. burn.) Fucking. Say. it. Through gritted
teeth.
Tell me, Poet. In a growl,
How your obligatorily human feelings eat you from the inside.
Like some parasite out of a sci-fi nightmare.
Tell *me *in *between *those *screeching *breaths you take to get
your point across as if we weren't already listening to you.
You feel like you gotta rub some drama on it, snap yo neck, spritz a
little sass, click yo tongue, get a little s a v a g e.
            Stop. Have a beer. You wanna shot?
It's our 7 dollars we paid to get through the door.
We're listening. We hear you. and if we're not, maybe we would
if we felt like you were being a little, fucking authentic.

39

**Headbang**

Classic question:
If you could live any part of history
which?
A music town. Maybe it's Seattle in the early 90s. Maybe it's London
in the 60s. Maybe it's Nashville just before country started to suck.
Wherever it is kinda doesn't matter.
I'd wanna be there when you realized that rhythmically bobbing
your head forward and back as some bass kicks, and some treble
flows,
and the fluctuation of a four-count unleashes feral freedom
inspiring feelings of fury, fornication and general fuckery.
I'd wanna live that moment.
A moment like that, you see
makes you wanna pay more attention to just how good you look
bedheaded, and galivanting in the moonlight.
Now, let's try to be honest (you should at least try to make an effort.)
The moment I'd wanna live in probably first took place in a drum
circle,
in the woods,
under a velvet sky,
studded with those beautiful diamond solitaires.
Let's try to be honest (you should try to make an effort, at least.)
it probably didn't happen in Nashville.

## Silicone Valley pomp & circumstance

Award shows. Pretending pomp, and premium content have some
sort of meaning.
They aren't "artists" they're "content creators" but you know what
Content is Cash
Content is King
That's the phrase right? Put a pretty face on a screen. Smear makeup
on it.
Let it tell you how to smear makeup on yourself.
Click. Click. Like. Subscribe. Blah blah blah.
Smash that notification bell.
or whatever.

## A full tank of gas

I often wonder,
more now, than when things were comfortable
If I went to get groceries. Got lunch, but instead of going back
to an apartment, in a city that feels cramped despite its
ego
I filled up at the gas station. Then took the nearest freeway
the 101, probably,
drove until I had to pick whether, or not to turn around and go back
to the apartment in the biggest small town you've ever lived in or
to drive through desert. A place I'm reluctant to call home, but still
feels so familiar.
(It's the heat probably)
What if I found out what was on the other side of that swath
of sand and warm colors that reminds me of a woman who had a
boat named after her.
(Yeah, she was like that)
I wonder where the trees start. I find myself missing trees.
I wonder how long it would take to hit the other coast.
Remember, if the water is now on your left, you're going south.
I wonder what it'd be like to spin off my fucken axis
concluding that since I have made it this far
I should probably just keep going.
I wonder if I sold my car, would it make me enough for a
*ahem*
"casual-one-way-fucking-off"
Across the ocean. Over indifferent currents.
I wonder if I'd be missed by the trees.
Or, if they were put there against their will,
would they grow out of spite for being stolen,
and envy me
for stealing their idea in the first place?

42

## Allow yourself

Disregard your apathy
Listen to an old song,
and let the warmth of the recording wrap your hardened heart.
Allow it to soften you for one moment.
Allow yourself a shiver,
a tear, that clogged feeling in your throat
when you know your dam is about to break,
and the roaring hurricane of emotion will over-take your
stubbornness.
Allow yourself to be human. Just for a moment.

## **Advice for the Young poet, contrary to Hank**

Create weird shit.
Get lost in another soul.
Realize that you have no one to blame but yourself.
Curse the life that was given to you.
Realize it's not so bad.
Get too drunk.
Get too high.
Realize you'd rather do both of those things than sit with a sweaty
piece of paper in your hand telling you you're next in line at the
DMV.
Wonder what the difference is between the DMV and a Butcher's
countertop
Ponder life.
Ponder death.
Ponder the pursuit of Sex, Drugs, and Rock and Roll.
Realize that when you're doing what you love, late at night by
candlelight,
life is Sex, Drugs, and Rock and Roll.
It is important that we do these things in our lifetime.
Though they are irrelevant, it is important that we do them.
Somebody told me they heard that once.
I'll let you know if she was right.
and I'll let you know if we get another shot.
And if we do, I'll tell you
don't try to make it better.
Only try to make it different.

## Go Outside. Fuck.

Why is the negligence of human beings invisible?
The death and decay of the good things in the world
is blocked behind a shiny wall of greed.
And thirty second fame. And a filter.
The rat race has changed.
Dance Monkey.
Clang those cymbals.
If you're loud enough someone might find the courage
to tell you to shut the fuck up.
Your government uses your toys to spy on you,
and sell you for pennies.
And we have the audacity to complain about life, liberty,
and someone fucking up our pursuit of sex, drugs, and rock and roll.
Get over how you think things are. Get over how you think
things happened.
Do some research instead. Don't follow the trends.
Put your toy down and go for a walk.
Brisk or not, doesn't matter.
Just something to get the blood moving to your brain.
Who knows.
You might like not getting so much attention.

## Relief

What a sweet relief
it is to have
outgrown things
that no longer inspire us

# III. A word about what love might be like

*based on the quantity of content*
*concerning the subject of the*
*next few pages,*
*it would appear that*
*I feel more strongly with*
*regards to the application of love*
*than I do about giving advice.*
*this is disconcerting.*

## **Notice:**

To the emotions it may concern,
The beatings will continue until morale improves.
Respectfully,

## Something Chemical Something Romance

I don't think "being in love" is all it's cracked up to be.
I think people just can't seem to handle the chemicals in their brain.
And I think
darkness turns sad into sweet, and the borderline perverse into the
outright arousing.
And I think
Envy is the sweet sting behind my teeth that turns a grimace into a
growl.

## Mistake(s)

There is something, though, isn't there?
about sitting in a pub, bar, coffee shop, park, tavern, nook, breakfast
table,
pen in hand, gliding over paper like it's what you were meant to do.
Remembering mostly by accident the hearts you've broken.
Because you weren't old enough, to have drunk enough,
to have made mistakes enough
to know what you were doing wasn't exactly what you needed,
but it was exactly what you wanted.
Mostly.
But you needed to make that mistake to know that it was wrong too.
And that's ok, because it's worth making the mistake to know better.

## Stinkfist

You're in North Hollywood, you want to be drifting,
But it's more of an enthusiastic skidding.
You want to be in a cooler car.
You want it to be like you're running from something.
But you're in North Hollywood.
And she's drunk riding shotgun, pounding on your dashboard
like she has any idea how to keep five-four time.
You're in a hatchback that you're going to wreck in a month
& you're running from jack shit.
But you drove, and her friends are making out in the back seat.
So, you might as well turn it up, cuz guess what?
This is gonna be the song that reminds you of her, no matter what.

## Strokes

One stroke. Two stroke.
Red stroke. Blue stroke.
Walk with me in the rain.
Pretend we're somewhere else.
Pretend this is all real.
Pretend we know exactly
what we're doing.
Pretend you can stare
at me without laughing,
And I'll pretend
that my thumbs aren't jealous
of the water droplets that
get to explore your cheek bones.

## Not if you don't

"Are you staring at me or the movie?"
she asks
and I have trouble telling her
that I really don't mind staring at her if she doesn't.

## Those killer flaws

Give me the broken things, shattered, torn, tossed aside,
Guess what? they're mine now.
I want frayed edges, smudged eyeliner,
a cigarette between pouty lips.
She might not know it. She might not feel it.
But it takes a certain amount of delicacy to hold one just like that.
A delicacy you can't pinpoint standing across the sidewalk.
And she doesn't care if you like it that way or not.

**Compromise**

Don't' tell me I was right,
shut up baby I know it,
but I'll never say I told you so

## Pain (thanks, I hate it)

Like something you can barely see.
Barely feel, like a breath on the back of the neck
in that moment nothing else matters.
Nothing else in the world.
Listening to them in the other room
or is it the refrigerator playing tricks.
Feels like you want to die.
But you try to write through it.
Because you're too high,
and you can't move anyway.
So, your pen moves for you.
"To feel the ocean (what) is to want to cease (the fuck) existence as
you know it.
To want the ocean (does this) is to want to sit in the dark (even
mean) with nothing."
and now, I know what it is to love tragically.
(thanks, I hate it)
By candlelight, indulging in perceived sighs, moans, screams,
shrieks of pleasure, makes for poetry, I suppose.

## I think I'll get that tattooed

What if the ink on my body isn't for me?
What if it isn't for you? Said the stars to the sky,
I lie
but I'm still burnt into your eyes,
if only (if only, the woodpecker sighs)
I could write a song that made the stars dance
if only if only
I could write a song that made the moon cry.

**4 am**

Look me in the eyes and tell me you love me.
Look me in the eyes and tell me
I'm awake because
I'm alive in your dreams.

## Violin song

Like a forgotten melody
So sweet. So sad.
Minor.
Major. But mostly minor.
I finally understand
why violinists make that face.
Because they create the songs.
that trees would sing.

## Terrible as the Dawn

I'm not looking for an angel,
But, the brightness of your wings
shatters my darkness.
Splintered into so many shards.
Well, maybe,
an angel with black wings
so I can get lost under the
beautiful canopy of her shadow.
That delicious darkness.
Yes. I want wings like blades.
Like so many knives.
Show me your edges, and
I'll show you parts of me tender enough to cut.

## Not if

but when
I die
I'd rather
relive
the moments
I laughed
until
I couldn't breathe
than go thru
another life
without them.

## Rage

I find myself
filled with hate, and, rage, and defiance.
The rise, and fall of friendships
into love and out again
the denial of all those things that made you seem weak.
You let that drawbridge down one time, and roll in that gift
that you believe is just for you,
but in the night your city burns, and falls, and shatters
crumbled into smoldering coals
and there's no one there to catch you,
or douse the flames
and so they consume you, and harden you
into something indestructible
Yeah, I fell in love once.
It was fucking awful,
and don't let anyone tell you otherwise.
If they do?
they're talking just to fill the space.

## Altruism

Everyone needs love.
Do not expect it to be returned.
But give empathy freely anyway.
We share
the same
unfortunate
condition of humanity.
Choose awareness over ignorance
and forgiveness over contempt.
I'll contradict myself in this.
I know.

**No might not always mean No**

She says she hates me,
but the way she asks for my touch
after I make her laugh
suggests the alternative.

*Hey, I had a great time with you in that mosh pit, wanna trip on psychedelics, and make art sometime?*

## Coming to grips

I won't change the world,
I can't.
but I may just inspire someone to change theirs

## Vanilla Silhouette

Soft growls.
Whiffs of a night spent making
poor
delicious
decisions
it'd be a travesty to forget
the events of a night that took place in clips
of creamy vanilla hewn silhouettes.
Moans in a low decibel
but a high frequency.
Be quiet. She'll say.
Ought not to arouse the neighbors
or their suspicions.

## Funny what good whisky can do

Inspiration through scotch,
fine tobacco
and a finer woman
none so fine as the Muse
who tells me I shouldn't play with fire.
Funny, I feel more like a wave,
crashing into whoever musters the courage
to stand in front of me and the ocean at my back.
So let me wash you
then watch me retreat.
Beckon me back for more.
Listen to how I sing.

Made in the USA
Monee, IL
30 July 2022

10528413R00049